YONDER

Kate Cumiskey

Silent E Publishing Company

Copyright © 2014 Kate Cumiskey

Silent E Publishing Company
4446 Hendricks Ave, #141
Jacksonville, FL 32207

ISBN-10: 0-9755104-9-5

ISBN-13: 978-0-9755104-9-0

1 2 3 4 5 6 7 8 9

ACKNOWLEDGMENTS

I am grateful to the following journals in which the poems listed previously appeared:

Blood Orange Review: Bioluminescence—luciferin catalyzed by luciferase

Cedars: Hawaiian Horses, Lessons from the Book of Ruth, Over Yonder, Septembers ago & Written in Little's Drugstore

Future Cycle: Pretty is as pretty does

Paterson Literary Review: 1971

Verse Wisconsin: Driving lessons & young

Zaum: Offering & Geometry in the madhouse

Thanks as well to Atlantic Center for the Arts for generous assistance with funds and time to—and gorgeous spaces in which to— work. Grants from the University of Central Florida and University of North Carolina, Wilmington, also gave me needed resources to complete these poems.

My incredible teachers and mentors, who formed my lyrical community: At UNCW—Mark Cox, Mark Doty, Clyde Edgerton, Philip Furia, Philip Gerard, Sarah Messer, Michael White; And, from that lovely space on Turnbull Bay, Atlantic Center for the Arts—Robert Creeley, Nick Flynn, Carolyn Kizer, and Peter Meinke.

Without the inimitable George Foote—nothing. Thank you George for the patience, intelligence, and careful crafting you've put into this book. You are a gift as a publisher and editor, but you are also kind.

I'm grateful to my partner, Mikel Cumiskey, who convinced me to write when we were still children; to our sons Mikel, Sam, Jacob, and James for fidelity and support. For this book, Terry Blackhawk, Peter Meinke, and Mark Cox have been generous with their time and words. A low bow to all.

Table of Contents

These poems are dedicated to my brother,
John D. Davis, my oldest friend.

Yonder *is not merely a Southern synonym for* there. *Yonder carries with it an inherent sense of distance farther than "there" and is used if the person or thing indicated can be seen. Or it might be nearby but completely out of sight, as in the next room.*

Pretty is as pretty does

Across two bridges, through the swamp, mangroves
poke stiff fingers at the low gray belly of dawn;
ivory and ash limbs bare across limitless green,
a constant changing murmur like lovers—
gray velvet wings of cranes whisper,
mullet splash, gators hiss then slap rising water.

I lean into November chill, my wet hair trailing
out the window all the way to school. Mother
said it was good for me, it built character, which
I waited for like the visit of some exotic relative
with tales of imagined things. I wanted
to be touched, to feel what other flesh
was like. To listen: patience even then
more a part of me than my own strange body.

Obedient, I waited for character to settle in,
wild cold hair a welcome mat. Patience...
Mother knew what was coming with her heavy,
mindless tasks— reeking
of bleach, calluses on my knees from scrubbing
the terrazzo floor while my mind *wandered*—
with her talk of what pretty girls do.
Answer: my skin is soft with rough, rough use.

Wishing for children, 1977, 1993

At that great art museum in New York, the one with *Peter Repentant* in the Rembrandt
Room; at the top of the stairway, second floor, hangs a picture of Salome reclining. Body
draped in golden cloth, ebony hair, voluptuous bowl of oranges by her couch; and at her
feet, a servant, a head on a platter. *That's* where I'd have you.

Oh, I envy Salome her devil-may-care sardonic air. What I wouldn't give. Instead
I'll take this hour alone to wish you ill: a cool, cloudy October afternoon on my own
chaise of boulders at the end of Sapphire Avenue, north of Mosquito Lagoon. Dead end.
Bottle green and faded red beach glass wink from the cove below. They could be broken
wishes you cast on an incoming tide, decades ago. Now, each time I give birth
you lose again, punishing yourself, insisting on being first in the room—stunned, after
Sam, by the mess, *did all of that come from you?* White as a ghost, bloodless as death.

Just there, gleaming in a bloody sunset on that rock black as pitch: the red-winged
blackbird, the coral snake. Which is which?

The only grandfather I ever knew

Ten good years, thirty of hell on Earth, ten more of heaven,
my grandmother said when she called to tell Mother she

thought my grandfather had died. Asked why she wasn't sure,
she replied, *he's still warm.* It was the first time she'd slept

next to him in ten years. Growing up, I thought everyone
had grandparents, one set. "Orphan" was not a word explained,

or mentioned. Somehow, both my parents seemed to belong
to Mama Kate and Papa Bill, who lived in the Sterling Street

house in Atlanta. *My* grandfather played tennis and danced,
never got good at collecting coal from beside the tracks.

His daughters found roundabout how he came to the city,
an uncle fetching him from Georgia Southern at seventeen,

dropping him outside the city limits, *Never come back.*
None of them know what he did. Verandahed galleries,

fine linen and privilege ghosted through his walk, in the tilt
of his head and direct blue gaze. He heard things in

chaotic conversations others didn't; listened, sedate
in his room from the high bed to grandchildren running

through the house on holidays, 1917 diploma yellowing
on the wall, silver watch tick-ticking on the dresser.

He never got used to working, hired again, again for his
photographic memory; fired again and again for the arrogance

of not showing. The only freight auditor to memorize tables,
he could name his price. Kate lost him constantly—on a rafting

trip down the Mississippi; a taxi ride from Atlanta to New Smyrna,
splendid and cool in white linen, in his summer fedora.

The interpreters
When it came night, the waves paced to and fro in the moonlight,
and the wind brought the sound of the great sea's voice to the
men on the shore, and they felt that they could then be interpreters.

--from 'The Open Boat', Stephen Crane

I

It was as though my father and the sea knew each other and learning
the language between them a matter of listening in the night to the ocean
speak.

Long summer evenings as the sun slipped past the far edge of the river
he took me over broken pavement, cool dunes, to the lacy hem of the sea;
let me feel the buoying of this water's salt. When I was *fish* enough to
handle surf any season, he brought me back. We watched sharks
feeding on bluefish in the slough.

Still so young I thought of time as a repeating circle between shoe days—
church on waking, dinner and nap, church before sleep—one night each
October my father woke me after my brothers, even Johnny who mostly
couldn't, slept.

I pulled jeans off the blue bed post, followed Dad out the side door. Light
pools under the lamps at Atlantic Avenue rustled with ghost-sounds
of palm fronds, just short of a keening, in the restless dark. The ocean
glowed—an inhuman skip and slide of moon, and other, light. Quicksilver
dolphin, barracuda, shark sheaths of life in waves.

II

We looked for turtles. The way to spot one is this: study a line of breaking
surf, *phosphorescence*, Dad called it, for a disruption in the necklace of light.
We'd stand on shore waiting while blackness became the slow pull of swollen
amphibian. She was—important to remember the *she* of this shape—slow,
aware of us the same way Mother kept her eyes on the babies all the while
her corn broom whisked sand from the broad terrazzo floor. I'd chatter. Then,
give in to sounds of the sea; lean against my father's leg until he lifted me.
I slept against his shoulder, only stirring at the intrusion of an occasional car
going north to the inlet. It was what we were there for, to steer lovers away
from turtles too low to be seen.

By morning it would seem a dream, the night-sea on my feet; musky smell
of pregnancy, sun-warmed hose water rinsing my ankles and feet, brush of
a towel. It might be. It might have been a dream.

III

In summer we slept in the Florida room, my brothers and me,
a step down from the kitchen; tall banks of jalousie windows cranked
flat. The beds lined up were neater than in their rooms other seasons;
stripes of solidarity in a quest for sleep. Four blond boys in brown
wooden single beds; and me on a cotton mattress atop open springs
too small for the frame, tied on with six loops of clothesline, half-hitched.

I'd lie on my side to watch Johnny in the next bed, wide amber eyes not
given over to envy, yet. I'd struggle to stay awake, couldn't understand
why sleep eluded him. Sometimes, when we were very small, I'd crawl
in next to him, hoping sleep would rub off. Mostly, sorry, my eyes slid
shut as tears slipped from his. I'd wake in the night to see his empty bed,
John on the terrazzo next to it, heat from his body leaching into stone.

Over yonder

Each October, my father & I woke in exactly the same humor. Mother
cried out against October—how she tolerated us, she'll never know.
Every morning, the ocean vindicated us.

Neither of us need see her to borrow that will, and on to our tasks.
Me to long division or algebra, he to his rockets. *Math and poetry*
have a lot in common, you know, is something he might be brave
enough to say right out loud, come October. In perfect synch,
we were masters of the house only then, those breezy days:
No one questioned us, just rolled their eyes, gritted their teeth.

And took it. Pedantic, misunderstood eleven months of the year,
our steps clipped with purpose, fairly dancing to our tasks, heady
with possibility. Everybody got out of the way.

I imagine he, too, was drawn to the water's edge over and over
that month, evenings—sometimes at dawn. The stir, stir, stir
of whitewash in the slough suggesting carnivorous life below
the surface, sometimes cresting.

As if the only order extant were natural, nothing manmade. As if,
as if. All we knew, he and I, underscored by the pincushioned slant
of sunlight from the horizon, off toward Africa. Sometimes God
sent a curl of exotic wood, wormeaten, salt-worn, to me—
from over yonder. My father said so. I believed him.

Yonder, too, was where his parents were; dying one then the other
like dreams in Mississippi mud—Uncle Ray making him drag
saplings for a log cabin under the chinaberry tree. Four years old;
making a place in the world only his, small orphan on a shelf under
quilts his mother had sewed. Sketching stars in the dust under that
tree when they came to tell him she was dead. Sometimes out
at the launch pad, checking an Apollo, the arms,

the white room, he felt them there—his parents, waiting beyond
sawgrass and salt flats, somewhere near the waves at Playalinda,
 just out of sight. He'd tell me those things, so I'd know—
comprehend the notions of time and distance in the spiritual realm,
impacting the physical, as if, as if, it were the most normal thing
in the Universe: *They are just yonder,* he'd say, pointing toward
Africa or maybe Venus, *as I will be, for you.*

For safety

A fight erupts outside the cafeteria door.
First, a *scree* not unlike the sound oozing
from a broken cat I found once. This sharpens
the chill in the air. Then
            someone shouts,
What happened to Cory?
He might have said, *yo' mamma,*
he might have said, *fat fuck.*

I felt safe in eighth grade behind concrete walls
three feet thick, four stories high—
we called it the jolly green giant. Solid
oak inner doors, transomed overhead to cool
classrooms. Teachers left windows open
all but the coldest days. And we all felt safer
there than at Coronado Elementary, only
an island closer to Castro's Cuba, ninety miles
past waves we could hear during quiet times, tests.
He was our threat.
            In kindergarten, we sat
under plate glass widows, hands spread over
our blond, blond heads, wondering if shadows
like us would be left after the blast.

What makes children feel safe? A few yards
of cement, rebar in walls? Underpaid adults wandering
halls with whistles, in bright yellow shirts?
Cameras on the bus?
            Canada? The deputy's car prowling the grounds,
his gun? No, Milwee is ten miles from here, and I confiscate
anything that even *appears* other than educational.
For safety.

My father used to say, *Every generation has its war.*
That puzzled me, he was never cynical. My brother,
the commander, has had six. What is happening, here?

Maxim

for Anna Schmidt

I pray for sons every time
I stand in the grocery aisle
looking at magazine covers.

Every time I pass clubs
where women strut for tips.

I pray weekday mornings
at 5:45, watching young girls
walk alone to the bus stop.

Every time I feel
a stranger's eyes slide
across my ass.

Anna, every time
my belly swells with life,
I sweat and pray for sons.

Lessons from the Book of Ruth
and Orpah kissed her mother-in-law; but Ruth clave unto her.
1:14

I.
Ruth
      clave

During famine she married him, as if
there might be happier times. She'd known
hunger; want, hands empty as a tomb.
      Married away,
           away
from her people. Stranger in an
empty land. Her clothes, her cloths
not purple, not silver; dun,
dust for a floor.
But his curls like chestnuts
in the sun, pressing,
promised other—her womb
folding glad as prayer awaiting
answer.
      Ruth never wavered
as Naomi buried them—
one husband, two sons. Dogged
tenacious as Jonah's gourd vine.
Orpah's kiss not betrayal,
not unexpected.
But this one, this daughter,
      kept.

II.
Orpah
      unto her gods.

gods like an old book, like the feel of canvas under thumbs rubbed
like cups, silver cups or tin filled and filled again
like beds of eiderdown and woolen robes wrapped round
like meat; meat roasting meat boiling meat dripping off bones
gods like fruit like olives pressed and sliding from the bowl
like grape seed staining flax like wine running rivers through

troughs of wine trenchers filled to the brim. Like that.
Orpah returned to gods like covers in the night like caves in winter
broad shade in desert sun like gold coins tinkling in a pocket
like lips like arms just at dawn like mist over the river rising
like mountains in front of the sun shining like children's voices
in song. Orpah kissed and returned, returned and kissed
her family of origin—her family, these years gone.

III.
Naomi
         wept again.

Bitter tears a mother losing one husband
two sons. And time slipped her grasp
rolling to the floor, ceased to matter.

No more sons, filling the door, littering
the floor with matter: no husband, hands
on the table, laughing at her burnt bread.

Famine wrapped round and through
turning, turning; every which way
a dervish of grief. A crisis of belief

so, letting the girls go back just progression.
The next step, as we step when covered
with the cloak of pain, no confession

left, no secret, no *sorry*!, no laugh.

Sight

She knows walls. Cool abrupt practical pain
of walls more forgiving than flesh. The first

time she saw that white space above where
the bed would go she saw herself splattered

there like sequins flung under water.
So she chose instead to think of stray

crayon marks, small prints in smudges
of finger paint. Living in that house three

years, choking, twisting from every mirror
she hated that wall. Before they moved

away he painted that bloodied place sweet
pink, covering well all of her, left there.

Geometry in the Madhouse

Just fifteen, but this is the safest place for her—
three bolted steel doors between Kathleen and parents
who come to blows over who must house &

feed her. In math, she said, *it's all right angles everywhere*
I look right angles wall parallel to wall books windows
tables! So she begged for an acute, even obtuse, one;

a leaning wall, a door ajar, a broken branch or a hand to hold.
Obsession allowed one terminus, the nurses were inflexible.
Don't worry, they crooned, *it's only a matter of degrees,*

and strapped her down, baring one round buttock for the straight
hot flush of stupor, her legs in leather locks a perfect V, slack
shoulders thirty degrees from bound wrists, from limp hands.

A new lump in Edna's remaining breast

They laugh the helpless laugh of women
knowing God: *what now, what now*
he does her, and all of us?

And they remember Edna twenty years ago
laughing, head thrown back, thick black hair
swinging. She is lovely, and loved:

it can't be helped. Nancy, of course,
is the difficult one—a McKenzie like
Mother—their aunt, and Edna their other aunt,

suddenly realized as a pair. Nothing changed,
just closed. Them, at twelve, recognizing
the *couple* Nancy and Edna, and now

on their knees to a God they firmly believe
will not abandon this woman.

An unexpected hour with my sister reveals nothing new

Waitresses don't like us. People in the restaurant watch us,
they think we're lovers. Our conversation is quick, disjointed—
but we follow. *We're not lunatics*, she says, knowing I am worried.
She tells me about discussing fears with a man. Hers are my own.
Institutions and being violent. Affirmatives I accept silently,
negatives I echo. *We won't be institutionalized.*
No, no we won't.

I think of my sister, who observed so much in silence, made herself
Invisible as she could. She is still, constantly, making herself small.
Still watching me, holding her body as still as she can,
wrapping tiny arms around her knees. She blends with the wall.
A friend stops to hug me. People turn to their eggs and toast
as she compliments my children & appearance. My sister feels
these remarks as if they were for her. She emerges a little
from the wall. If I am careful now, don't speak of her,

I can draw her out as I did when she was a child.
I can make her safe.

After brain surgery

Since I have been back
you cling to me as you
have not done since
moments after your birth.

Calmed only by my generic
presence, it's a wanting
in you easily met.

Since I am too weak,
 you make a game
of holding on alone. Strong
legs embrace my waist.
Hands light
on my shoulders, you
never touch the inverted
U of closure on the back
of my head where I hold
pain, in tissue
that will not multiply.

How do your piano
fingers know to play
on my face as you press
your lips together, intent,
and kiss me
            over and over?

Bioluminescence—luciferin catalyzed by luciferase
   --a found poem
            after Jason Roberts

Luminous beings, rare above the waterline
(fireflies, angels) are ubiquitous below.
Shrimp, threatened, release a blinding
cloud of light as octopi do ink:
in obscurity lies escape.

The fleshy beacon
of anglerfish entice
not prey but mates, who wear
light in spangled bands.

We think we understand
but don't—
light that dispels only darkness,
gives no warmth.

We are the unspangled, unglowing, thick
and mute and dark whose attempts
to engage it are lost on this lovely light.

Poem for my brother, John

You and I leave the bus at a dead run down Robinson Road;
you grab the tackle while I whip off dress and cotton slip, slide
into jeans. Identical in our undershirts and Keds, down
Peninsula, past Sapphire, Condict, Normandy, through the light
at Flagler we pedal hard, the bait bucket and cane poles thwacking
our knees, down to Red's Bait under live oaks dripping Spanish moss.

Ten cents a dozen for live shrimp, a nickel for a Coke, fingertips
numb from digging in the red and white steel cooler. Good
to be a girl if shrimpers are around, I tilt my head, grin,
and get one for free. Bucket heavy on the handlebars, musky
sweet water sloshing through the air holes, we head for the pier
at Due East. It's usually our own. Today an old woman
pulling in fingerlings with a cast net shows us to *hook them
 through the tail, snappers like 'em head first.* We catch an even
dozen, and you let me pass the stringer through velvet red gills
moving slow as the salty air in my lungs. I watch the fish
hang, tired now, by the piling and just stand, safe, near you.

The migratory patterns of North American birds

John spent the summer before seventh grade studying the migratory
patterns of North American birds. I followed after as always, watching,

his knowledge my gospel. He fed me misinformation, sometimes,
but that summer, too hot for joking, required focus. Instead of fishing

from rocks along the river or traipsing dunes for crab holes, we spent
long mornings in the library, the coldest building in town. Father gave

him a pad of onionskin paper; he began at the back, first in pencil, then
marker, heavy black outlines of states curving up through empty pages

like a promise. At noon, we pedaled home over two bridges, a causeway;
cottony egrets calling from the mangroves, blue and gray herons statues

along the margins. Devoted to his task, John worked through the hottest
 part of the day me nodding beside him while Mother and the babies slept,

air around us viscous with humidity. I'd wake to peer at scattered pastel
pencils, opened books, John bent over a page charting the path of the red-

winged blackbird, a new crease etching the skin between his eyes. His
eyes, amber cat eyes moving between page and pencil with intensity I'd

never share. Each week, a new page complete; colored lines magical rivers
flowing south. In late August he discovered the path of the brown pelican,

heading for shallow Gulf waters, led directly over our backyard. One windy
afternoon, months after abandoning me at Coronado Elementary for Junior

High, John flew in the door, dropped his books and rushed me outside. They
were so close I could see separate feathers, cream and mottled tan, on tender,

fattened bellies. For days they flocked in such flawless formations, John
explained, the lead bird— maybe the second two—need only dip their left

wings to change the current of air rising from earth in the corner of the yard,
leading the flock easily out to sea. I never doubted him for a moment. For years

after, I stood there on October afternoons watching the same birds, I swear,
glide twenty feet overhead. And still sometimes I look up to see an impossibly

thin pastel path etching the air, leading from John, in Far Rockaway, to me.

Sunday Dinner

At Norwood's Restaurant, the power-room door was pink.
Each thick glass tabletop cover a white, white sand beach;
miniature dunes preserved in time-out-of-mind; shells clumped
as if, just beyond the glass-topped box, waves rolled ready

to tumble them back to the ocean floor. A few blades of seagrass,
a gold coin. And high above, fans hung on poles tall, pencil thin;
tobacco dark old men. I liked the long table by the window
best. Its shells were the exact colors of sunlight on the gentle heads

of my brothers. After Sunday dinner, face tilted up near the counter
I smelled smoked mullet Father bought when he paid the bill, a treat
that turned Mother coy and quiet all the rest of the day. For me,
Butter Rum Lifesavers from a rack like bleachers at the ball park.

There, too, were blue and white rolls, shining packs of gum.
I held my golden candy in the curl of my tongue all the lazy
way home in the back-back of the station wagon, head drooping,
heavy, pungent as a magnolia blossom on John's thin shoulder.

Poem to a second child
for Sam

Someday when I fold this shirt
it will be faded and seem so small;
I will have a vague memory of today,
that it was a good day and at the end of it
I stood here folding, watching you watch TV.

Now, the shirt is new and bright. I am careful
to handle it just so because when we bought it
you were happy, finally all ready
for the first day of school, telling
me how much you already know,
how lucky they'll be
to have you there.

Headlong

Mother swears it was her that burnt me, but my guilt's implied,
Bolting through the kitchen in just your underwear—but a shirt
would have trapped the syrup from that pot of carrots I ran
headlong into. All I remember is my father's face over the bathtub,
when he'd scrub dead skin away: *Tilt your chin up I'll try not
to hurt you I'm sorry I'm sorry.* That scar is so old it might as well
be sun damage.

After, trapped in fire dreams, for years my howls brought
the whole house running—I had to choose which to save:
The baby, or a basket of kittens nursing in the foot
of Mother's closet, behind her dresses.

I learned to be cagy, come bath time. Beyond dotting the insides
of her wrists with baby milk, she never had time for the nuances
of temperature.

Count the candles on that cake, John said when he called last
Sunday. I hoped he'd focus on my white-blond hair or gleaming
almond eyes peeking over the easy-bake oven, my birthday
present. Or, maybe the car hood the cake rested on, Bill's $200
Corvair with a huge red and blue peace sign spray-painted
on the trunk. Dad drove it to the Cape year after year,
Best car we ever had.

John could always see what I miss: four white candles shining
in November afternoon behind me, just four, and laughs,
*we had to use that thing on the driveway so we wouldn't burn
the house down.*

Mother gave us biscuit dough when we ran out of paper packets
of cake mix and we squatted on the cement, ruining our dinners.
I feel the singe of metal trays on my fingertips—
I *knew* about conduction, got faster.

Driving lessons

I'll never be able to do this, I said, watching Kurt navigate
the left from Flagler onto Peninsula, palming the wheel
of his Dad's Olds through a curve smooth as the small
of my back when he kissed me. *You,* he laughed, right
arm stretched behind me along the seatback, *will be
a wonderful driver.* The next day he dropped me the keys
as I stood obedient and patient as a spaniel at the foot
of the lifeguard tower. *Back it above the tideline. Wait
for traffic, then just take your foot off the brake.
Don't get stuck.*

Two years later, Mother taught me to drive in the unfinished
parking lot of the new Publix Supermarket. She used
the Chevy wagon instead of the Fiesta. *Might as well learn
to handle it now.* It's the main thing I remember learning
from her. Dad taught me to sing, to read, celestial navigation.
Your Daddy, she said, *is a terrible driver. He learned on
a farm. I took my father to work in Atlanta when I was twelve.*
After a week or so of parking lots and the short streets
of the island, she handed me the keys to the stick shift.
Go to work. Take your brother, first. John drove, got out,
leaned in and said, *Take the North Bridge, for heaven's
sake. What's the worst that can happen.*

I taught my husband to drive. This is what he tells me,
but none of my memories of him in cars involve driving
lessons. *We were eighteen. How could you forget that?*
I recall parking in the Fiesta in broad daylight by the side
of Dune Circle, kissing for hours, and John's insistent fist
banging on the back window of the Chevy at three in
the morning, Mikel and I stoned out of our minds. *Get
dressed. Now. We'll tell Mother you got stuck, couldn't
leave the car. You were frightened of the rising tide.*

Clint Eastwood
for Robert Creeley

He
        shows up
(sometimes)
at the Hog's Breath.
Most times he
        doesn't.

In Carmel, there are
no stop signs.
The most
                expensive
car goes
        first.

You could sit
all day
        in a Subaru
going
                nowhere.

young

--after Robert Creeley

all
they needed
was the mattress
on the floor
and stipples
of sunlight
texturing a
  New World:
    heart pine,
    flesh, flecks
    of salt
    sparkling
    in air.

Three children later

He wanted her enough that when her father said,
Get a real job, son, never believing he would,
the boy shaved his head, swore an oath, and off

they went, laughing. They stayed on base
for entertainment, the living room huge, empty;
they bounced checks for food. He bought

her yard sale skates just to watch, and jogged
easily behind. That tour of duty passed as gently
as the sunlit blond from her hair. Still, he touches

her as if he is dipping his fingers in holy water,
thinking, *This is mine, but, for the life of me,
I don't know why.*

Silver anniversary poem

I could have had you sooner, but then,
I might not have you now. It was raining

the night you teased *Kiss me, or sit here
alone.* I loved that heavy rain like a warm

velvet curtain but not the parking lot. So,
lifting my face (afraid of being swallowed

whole) your mouth bloomed on mine. Trying
to recall other kisses, there were none.

I think I married you then. You knew exactly
what you were doing. Timing is everything.

Mother

The afternoon you snapped, *Just where have you been
all day, young lady?* and I replied, *Right here beside you—*
here being the ICU waiting room we'd pretty much
commandeered weeks before—was the day I realized
there was no more I could do for you.

Easy to do for Daddy, the sick one; always some chore
to be done. But nothing for the one who loves and is left
and suddenly I understood all those who do not love:
brilliant women who choose stupid men,
relatives which never call.

For a love like yours, five decades, three homes, seven
children & one dying, is almost unendurable. And when
I saw you bend to shamelessly kiss his sleeping lips
over and over in the next days as you had never done
in front of me before, I knew you were sending him

ahead in this journey with a selfless and broken heart
I hadn't yet earned the right to witness, but couldn't look
away.

Tenacious Kate:
      for Kate Mills McKenzie

left me two sewing baskets
a hand mirror a gold ring
and a name.

spent her sixth summer in an iron lung
made it sound like a social club
      Oh lots of us there that year.

stood four eleven in stocking feet
never raised her voice
ruled that house with what her
daughters called an iron hand.

bought stockings and a garter belt
one summer and sent me home
with a tea kettle for Mother and
a passion for black pumps
      no stockings no kettle
never could tell Anne a thing.

sold the house in Decatur
to buy cancer treatments
for Whilhelmina Louise,
and rented for the rest of her life.

stalled the Buick at Little Five Points
climbed off her phone book tapped
the window of the man behind
      You go start my car—
I'll be happy to lean on that horn
until you get back.

drove over the base of a massive oak
already half blind from a tumor threading
like a spider through her occipital lobe.

lied from her nest of pillows that she
could see the TV (just sound and snow)
just fine, and shooed Carolyn and Nancy out
when they came to check on her:
     I'm just enjoying listening
to my girls out in the kitchen.

Apologies for an oldest child

I should have praised you,

but you were the first, child
of children rushing to create.
I should have let you throw cereal
& laugh, put your fat feet
on the table to kiss.
There is a picture of your
first birthday. You are bending
to the cake, no fork, careful
hands held out of the way,
rosy lips tentative.

Mikel Jon, I was so young:
I should have let you be.

Offering

Your brother left a mango on the scarred face
of the worktable. *Eat it today,*
he told you, staying only a moment.

I arrive home to learn you've never had one;
married sixteen years in April, you
are a mango virgin.

Its colors slide across my palms;
the magenta and golden skin enjoys
an Indian summer. By midnight

I am beyond ready to slip through
the slumbering house, past the humming
refrigerator, the nightlight, to pick up

this token and warm it against my chest.
You are right where I want you, sprawled
out contemplating sleep when I open

the fruit whose juices drip
slick, sweet as my own,
over your lips, your fingertips.

Return to New Smyrna

You went at it like that, full tilt, hard—
smoking down to your fingers then
Thumbing the roach in your pocket.
The sky would never fall;
even the wind befriended you.

Red shorts stiff with yesterday's
salt, blazoned lifesaving patch to rub.
Sand under your flesh, morning
biscuit—even the dew a throbbing, returning
constant. And the sea always welcomed you,
no matter the hour, no matter the form—

smooth and clear as glass or thrashing—
you went at it; like that, full tilt,
so hard, the sky would never fall.
Even the wind befriended you.

Four in the fire

In each of the paintings she sees Christ.
He sees a—usually large—penis, depending
on the canvas and color dripped

like nectar around figures not burning.
Over for dinner, he teases her about it,
can't believe she's bought Shadrach,

Meshach, and Abednego, cooled in the furnace
by the son of Daniel's God gliding eternal
down this painted prison. He stares at them—

the slashes of color, Nebuchadnezzar's
child-prisoners *savant*, unbowing, in whom
there is no blemish, well-favored,

skillful in all wisdom, understanding
science; having ability to stand
in the king's palace and teach.

Redemption

Philip is straight and neat. Brilliant and clean—
all black and white against shades of gray. At fifteen
he said he was going ROTC because there'd be some war
maybe a draft while he was eligible and he preferred to be
the one sending troops in, saving them; not a lamb
to slaughter. He's been through six wars. *Six wars.*

From the Gulf he sent taped diaries home, voice hushed
in the dead hours, long spaces of the hum of watching
between words. Officer of the deck when the order came
to launch missiles into Baghdad, Lieutenant jg Philip Davis
earned a Navy Achievement Medal. A nam.*

The only conservative out of seven siblings, Philip stood splendid,
arrow-straight in his whites in our parents living room, the September
morning the world blew apart. For our father's funeral I'd asked him
to wear them—we were all suddenly glad he did, but that didn't stop
the screaming tirade from the rest of us; rage, rage against
the machine, until someone said, *He's Philip's Commander
-in-Chief. There's a good chance he'll be called, today. Save it.*

My brother found Jesus in a fundamentalist storefront church,
and one Norfolk noon a man strolled into the packed rec room
with a grenade—lonely sailors shooting pool, ripe for redemption—
and, hand on pin, stood forty-five minutes listening to the *hush*
in Philip's voice, hum of calm between words.

   **the kind of award other sailors comment on in airports.*

What it is about an eight year old
for Adam Walsh

is he'll believe everything you tell him. When she points out
the woodpecker near the base of the oak outside the kitchen window
 keeping time with the stereo he says, "let's see how he does with
the one the dog loves." And his lips move, long toes tap, tap linoleum
managing a groove between the red-crested head and Ray Davies'
sliding croon. She lets him play it as many times as he wants, because
he is eight, because he can manage the volume by himself. He knows
what the bird is after, the burrowers hidden in the trunk and could recite
their proper and fanciful names.

She lets him go out the back door
>*the hardest thing, the hardest thing she does*
>*letting one of the children out of sight*
and around the house to stand watching, still dancing a bit, long white
fingers waving at particles of spring drifting through town.
>*it was an oak she stood under, the daycare closed*
dark and empty in the cold Spring night

If she's done her work well, at this point he believes he can do anything.
Because she has given him the song and the bird, he lets her pick the book.
Lets her climb to the top bunk, plump pillows and trip and tumble over
Amelia Bedelia,the wide sky of his eyes, the not-quite-fit of new front teeth
folded hands
>*like his brother, the one taken and miraculously returned;*
>*and she tastes the week vanished twenty years ago like bile rising*
almost too much to take.

Understand this: that until the sapling wrists thicken, until his boy smell
sharpens into something singular and foreign, she'll breathe shallow—
until trust fades into the reality of a world that lets eight year olds vanish
from the toy aisle of the local Sears.

one answer
after Sally Smits

As if when, that night in Gainesville walking
home from the laundromat, Mikel, four, skipping
beside me asked,
            What's destiny?

And, after my stumbling reply, *Can your destiny
change mine?,* I could put my arms around
motherhood like curving next to him
the night he was born, his scent the secret
            of my womb.

Too late to reconsider, his question dropped me
from a platform of certainty into a well of love,
so when he calls from a stop in his journey
the word *homeless* propels me

to pour money on the counter of an all-night
Western Union office, a pilgrim before the altar.
How can I not rescue my issue, my flesh despairing,
three thousand two hundred seventeen
            miles from home?

Destiny, I hear, squeeze my eyes tight as his father
breathes even in the bed beside me,
and bend to press my
            lips to impossible

softness of the shadow of that downy shape:
flesh of our flesh, bone of our bones,
            between us.

davidjohnchristopherandjoan

There's an old woman in a wheelchair
in the icy fall sunlight near the atrium wall.
Hands clasped beneath her chin, the fingers
of the right twist an imagined ring round
and round on the third finger of the left.
Her gaze, washed-out blue, stares past
two others sitting by, and all the nurses
hurrying past, the words she repeats
like a mantra the only thing—and the ring—
keeping her here:

Shy boy, gone too soon
for Bob Creeley

I'm certain my father finally made it to Venus.
About you, I can only be sure of this—
you were *terrified. Scared to death.*

And I—lamer than you,
tendering the eye—
could only offer my two
close brushes, that secondhand
peace.

How can such energy just *end?*

If only Jason & I had cleaned those
front porch rocker runners...
No matter. Done is done.

I still feel the unexpected press
of your lips on my cheek;
strong, young as your hip lingo, *Dig it,*
        and hear
beautiful Penelope's delighted laugh.

How
you quickened beside me
moments before,
spotting her in the parking lot.
Almost crashing to the pavement
in your eagerness. Almost.

Septembers ago

Sometimes I see you in that horrible physical therapy room
at the place called Rehab in the Temporary ward of Oceanview
Nursing home: a place for dying. After you used up your energy
and nearly all your heart traversing the long hall, proud

and stubborn with the aluminum walker, sitting down behind
that ridiculous wheel with pedals should have been a relief.
Instead, you couldn't get a word in edgewise with the therapist
who talked at you like you were four; *Come on, Mr. Davis, you*

can do it, come on now! You were thinking, *Lunkhead, I haven't*
pedaled a bike in sixty years, sixty years. But you hesitated,
picking your battles. And gave up. Then I realized you knew
we were almost there. So we let the idiot babble as I bent down,

picked up each of your slippered feet in turn, one hand under
an arch, one behind a knee, put them on the pedals and gave
the wheel a shove so he'd go away. I sat behind you, placed
my arms around you and gripped your hands like you did mine,

so many Septembers ago, lifting me up over the waves, swinging
me out from you for the sheer joy of it: everything flying but you,
strong and brown and solid in the ocean, pointing me out to sea.

1971

And if we could reach inside ourselves, open our hearts
and let all that darkness go, would we? I'd return with you
to the Hueytown woods, carry your terrors into adulthood.
We did what we could. I found a cat one summer evening

broken, keening—you were the brother who knelt,
took the string from your left shoe, deliberate, while
I stood behind and watched your back expand and
contract with silent sobs. Your hands never shook

but your blue eyes were terrible all the way home.
You hid me behind the kitchen counter the night
Rusty spent across town in a cell, strung out on horse.
Our parents cried at the table until dawn. When he left

to hop a freight for anywhere, it seemed Mother left, too,
returning on Sunday evenings after his call, for an hour
or so. I'd wait in his neatly made bunk for that ring, willing
him alive with nine-year-old logic for her, just for her, by staring

at blue meanies he'd painted on the wall. So it was you
who took over, checked our homework, bandaged our wounds.
When did your sweetness go bitter? Now I am the enemy,
my messy, abundant life. You once asked, *If this is twins,*

can I have one? I swallowed the knowledge that it had been
and gave the surviving child your name. Perhaps our finest
hour will have to be last night in the mangrove swamp,
speaking of nothing. Your cigarette the only unnatural light,

bioluminescence popped through the water with every
lazy cast and into the silence I thought, *Peace be with you,*
when you said, *There's a poem here.* It wouldn't be what
you expected. Nothing ever will.

Hawaiian horses

I build a poem around your horses then
begin again: you & me with columbine, seersucker,
Perky the parakeet hiding in jackets. After

I'll take you out for ice cream. Anything you want—
if wishes were horses, beggars would ride, your grandmother
used to say. I never knew what she meant until now,

watching your new wife's granny skip and dance down
the aisle on Jordan's arm as if there is a chance for you, 67
years behind her. The San Juans beckon beyond opened

French doors of the community hall: American flag above
chafing dishes, your father and I, breathless. Take me
to your horses, blind or demented. Whatever my gloaming brings.

Lift me to their velvet backs & let me lean down to whisper
knowing at least something was given in all the chaos.
Your pictures, my diphthongs; *ah* of me: *chi*, you.

Anniversary of the death of a Mississippi orphan

Tomorrow at 2:24 in the afternoon you'll have been dead
six months. For reasons I can't unravel I make butter.

That was your job, churning for hours on your grandmother's
porch while your father lay upstairs, weakening with high sugar.
I see you there, solemn child never complaining, little arms
straining, straining. Down the hill, the springhouse whispers.

I improvise, using Jimmy's soup thermos half-filled
with heavy cream. You'd be pleased at your own reflected
 ingenuity. We have made a lasagna; Mikel started the sauce
at ten, not your tomatoes but they'll do. He goes out

for flowers and a tin, slices apples and I toss them.
The cinnamon and sugar act as a balm against my skin.
Off and on, I shake butter, in my wrists the ache
of little boy hands. Beyond the window Venus rises.

I'm in no hurry and children scurry about. Why do I make
butter? It will not bring you back or honor the rocket scientist
I knew. Perhaps to comfort the child on that porch who
will lose so much, who will never, never complain.

I knew you best those weeks before death washing your hands
and face tucking you in like you tucked each of the seven of us.
Sheet squared and turned over the blanket at the neck
for maximum warmth, maximum softness.

In I.C.U. you whispered, *Because my parents took
such good care—because they loved me so— my only worry
was hurting their feelings by rumpling the covers.*

So, thirsty for spring water, I make butter then feed it on crackers
to Mikel. *It's the sweetest thing*, he says, *I've ever tasted.*

Written in Little's Drugstore

A green cart of cantaloupe
under a fat Florida sky
waiting for three o'clock rain.

www.ingramcontent.com/pod-product-compliance
Lightning Source LLC
Chambersburg PA
CBHW062109090426
42741CB00015B/3368